C#.NET AND THE WPF LISTVIEW

Using WMI to power the Listview

Richard Thomas Edwards

INTRODUCTION

Get ready to learn something new

Wheathter you are a seasoned pro working with the WPF ListView or a newbie trying to figure out how to use it, you ether know the WPF ListView has a learning curve. And to be perfectly honest, it is not ready for programming it when added to the WPF Application. In-other-words, it is configured wrong when it is automatically added from the toolbox with a double click.

This is the initial XML tag with the default settings:

```
<ListView Height="100" HorizontalAlignment="Left"
Margin="10,10,0,0" Name="listView1" VerticalAlignment="Top"
Width="120" />
```

This is what you see:

To make the ListView auto resize:

```
<ListView Height="auto" HorizontalAlignment="stretch"
Name="listView1" VerticalAlignment="Stretch" Width="auto" />
```

This is the result:

```
┌─────────────────────────────────────────────────────────────┐
│ ▣  MainWindow                              —    □    ×        │
├─────────────────────────────────────────────────────────────┤
│                                                               │
│                                                               │
│                                                               │
│                                                               │
│                                                               │
│                                                               │
│                                                               │
│                                                               │
│                                                               │
│                                                               │
│                                                               │
│                                                               │
│                                                               │
└─────────────────────────────────────────────────────────────┘
```

There is one mode that needs to be discussed. That is `<ListView.View>`

So, I added a couple of columns:

```
        <ListView Height="Auto" HorizontalAlignment="Stretch"
Name="listView1" VerticalAlignment="Stretch" Width="Auto">
            <ListView.View>
                <GridView>
                    <GridViewColumn
Header="ProductID"></GridViewColumn>
                    <GridViewColumn
Header="ProductName"></GridViewColumn>
                </GridView>
            </ListView.View>
        </ListView>
```

The ListView now looks like this:

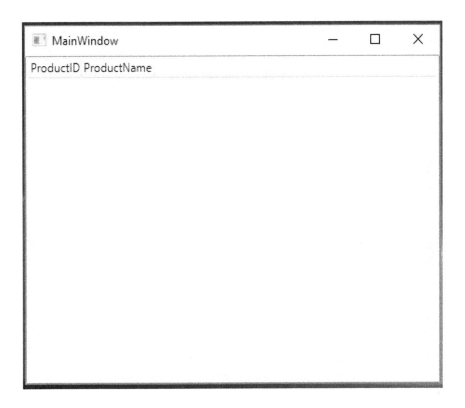

What happens if I take something like the DataTable add, the column names and gave it a couple of values?

```
DataTable dt = new DataTable();
dt.Columns.Add("ProductID");
dt.Columns.Add("ProductName");

dt.Rows.Add();
dt.Rows[0][0] = "1";
dt.Rows[0][1] = "Peanut Brittle";
```

```
listView1.DataContext = dt;
```

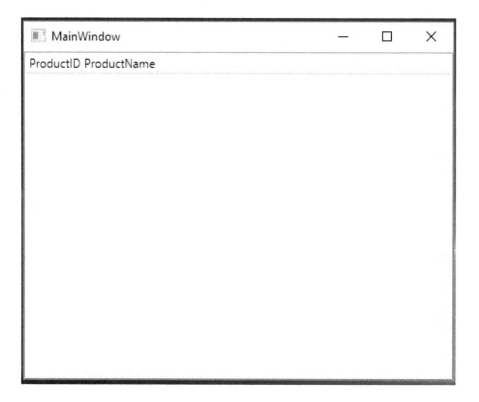

Well that didn't work, did it? Okay so, let's try ItemsSource instead.

```
DataTable dt = new DataTable();
dt.Columns.Add("ProductID");
dt.Columns.Add("ProductName");

dt.Rows.Add();
dt.Rows[0][0] = "1";
dt.Rows[0][1] = "Peanut Brittle";


listView1.ItemsSource = dt.DefaultView;
```

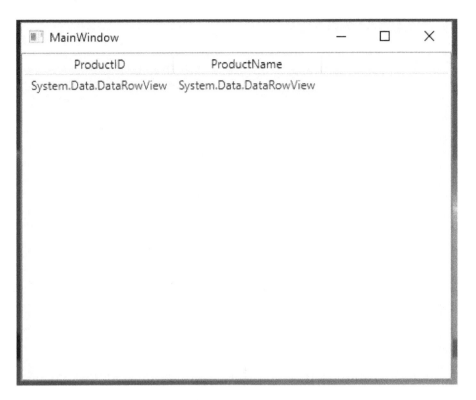

Well now there is something there but not showing.

```
DataTable dt = new DataTable();
dt.Columns.Add("ProductID");
dt.Columns.Add("ProductName");

dt.Rows.Add();
dt.Rows[0][0] = "1";
dt.Rows[0][1] = "Peanut Brittle";


listView1.ItemsSource = dt.DefaultView;
```

Well that kind of worked. What are we missing?

This is what was missing:

```
<ListView Height="Auto" HorizontalAlignment="Stretch"
Name="listView1" VerticalAlignment="Stretch" Width="Auto">
    <ListView.View>
        <GridView>
            <GridViewColumn Header="ProductID"
DisplayMemberBinding="{Binding ProductID}"></GridViewColumn>
            <GridViewColumn Header="ProductName"
DisplayMemberBinding="{Binding ProductName}"></GridViewColumn>
        </GridView>
    </ListView.View>
</ListView>
```

Once DisplayMemberBinding is set and we use our example code:

```
DataTable dt = new DataTable();
dt.Columns.Add("ProductID");
dt.Columns.Add("ProductName");

dt.Rows.Add();
dt.Rows[0][0] = "1";
dt.Rows[0][1] = "Peanut Brittle";


listView1.ItemsSource = dt.DefaultView;
```

We get this:

All well and good, but does this also work with the DataContext?

```xml
<ListView Height="Auto" HorizontalAlignment="Stretch"
Name="listView1" VerticalAlignment="Stretch" Width="Auto">
        <ListView.View>
            <GridView>
                <GridViewColumn Header="ProductID"
DisplayMemberBinding="{Binding ProductID}"></GridViewColumn>
                <GridViewColumn Header="ProductName"
DisplayMemberBinding="{Binding ProductName}"></GridViewColumn>
            </GridView>
        </ListView.View>
    </ListView>
```

Once DisplayMemberBinding is set and we use our example code:

```
DataTable dt = new DataTable();
dt.Columns.Add("ProductID");
dt.Columns.Add("ProductName");

dt.Rows.Add();
dt.Rows[0][0] = "1";
dt.Rows[0][1] = "Peanut Brittle";


listView1.DataContext = dt;
```

▪ MainWindow	— □ ✕
ProductID ProductName	

What happens when we also set the ItemsSource = {Binding} ?

```
<ListView Height="Auto" HorizontalAlignment="Stretch"
Name="listView1" VerticalAlignment="Stretch" Width="Auto"
ItemsSource="{Binding}">
        <ListView.View>
            <GridView>
                <GridViewColumn Header="ProductID"
DisplayMemberBinding="{Binding ProductID}"></GridViewColumn>
                <GridViewColumn Header="ProductName"
DisplayMemberBinding="{Binding ProductName}"></GridViewColumn>
            </GridView>
        </ListView.View>
    </ListView>
```

And the code:

```
DataTable dt = new DataTable();
dt.Columns.Add("ProductID");
dt.Columns.Add("ProductName");

dt.Rows.Add();
dt.Rows[0][0] = "1";
dt.Rows[0][1] = "Peanut Brittle";

listView1.DataContext = dt;
```

ProductID	ProductName
1	Peanut Brittle

MANUALLY POPULATING THE LISTVIEW THROUGH CODE

The first thing we're going to do here is to create a solution to a problem I have not seen on the internet as solving the persistence of the name value pair. But before we go resolving that, let's resolve the first issue.

To create a usable column, we have to do this:

```
GridView gv = new GridView();
Binding bi = null;
GridViewColumn c = null;

bi = new Binding("ProductID");
c = new GridViewColumn();
c.Header = "ProductID";
c.DisplayMemberBinding = bi;
gv.Columns.Add(c);

bi = new Binding("ProductName");
c = new GridViewColumn();
c.Header = "ProductName";
c.DisplayMemberBinding = bi;
gv.Columns.Add(c);
```

```
DataTable dt = new DataTable();
dt.Columns.Add("ProductID");
dt.Columns.Add("ProductName");

dt.Rows.Add();
dt.Rows[0][0] = "1";
dt.Rows[0][1] = "Peanut Brittle";

listView1.View = gv;
listView1.ItemsSource = dt.DefaultView;
```

This, of course, works perfectly fine.

But what happens when we want to use the DataContext?

```
GridView gv = new GridView();
Binding bi = null;
```

```
GridViewColumn c = null;

bi = new Binding("ProductID");
c = new GridViewColumn();
c.Header = "ProductID";
c.DisplayMemberBinding = bi;
gv.Columns.Add(c);

bi = new Binding("ProductName");
c = new GridViewColumn();
c.Header = "ProductName";
c.DisplayMemberBinding = bi;
gv.Columns.Add(c);


DataTable dt = new DataTable();
dt.Columns.Add("ProductID");
dt.Columns.Add("ProductName");

dt.Rows.Add();
dt.Rows[0][0] = "1";
dt.Rows[0][1] = "Peanut Brittle";

listView1.View = gv;
listView1.ItemsSource = dt.DefaultView;
```

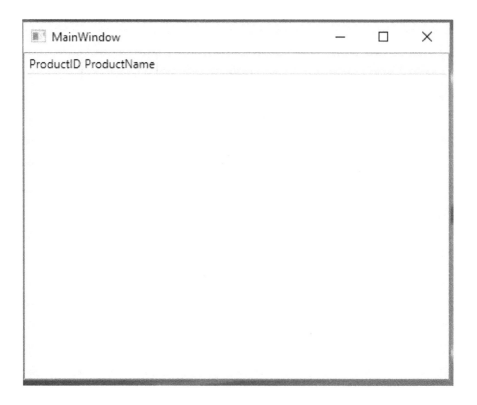

We're back to nothing. And this could be a hassle.

```
GridView gv = new GridView();
Binding bi = null;
GridViewColumn c = null;

bi = new Binding("ProductID");
c = new GridViewColumn();
c.Header = "ProductID";
c.DisplayMemberBinding = bi;
gv.Columns.Add(c);

bi = new Binding("ProductName");
c = new GridViewColumn();
c.Header = "ProductName";
c.DisplayMemberBinding = bi;
gv.Columns.Add(c);
```

```
DataTable dt = new DataTable();
dt.Columns.Add("ProductID");
dt.Columns.Add("ProductName");

dt.Rows.Add();
dt.Rows[0][0] = "1";
dt.Rows[0][1] = "Peanut Brittle";


listView1.DataContext = dt;
```

We're back to nothing, again, right? Turns out, you do have to add the ItemsSource to the attributes list of the ListView:

```
<ListView Height="Auto" HorizontalAlignment="Stretch"
Name="listView1" VerticalAlignment="Stretch" Width="Auto"
ItemsSource="{Binding}"/>
            GridView gv = new GridView();
```

```
Binding bi = null;
GridViewColumn c = null;

bi = new Binding("ProductID");
c = new GridViewColumn();
c.Header = "ProductID";
c.DisplayMemberBinding = bi;
gv.Columns.Add(c);

bi = new Binding("ProductName");
c = new GridViewColumn();
c.Header = "ProductName";
c.DisplayMemberBinding = bi;
gv.Columns.Add(c);


DataTable dt = new DataTable();
dt.Columns.Add("ProductID");
dt.Columns.Add("ProductName");

dt.Rows.Add();
dt.Rows[0][0] = "1";
dt.Rows[0][1] = "Peanut Brittle";


listView1.View = gv;
listView1.DataContext = dt;
```

And that produces this:

ProductID	ProductName
1	Peanut Brittle

Okay, let's get back to using something else other than a DataTable

As with VB.Net and C#.Net – okay, I am sure there are others – there is the concept of a structure. But in C#.Net, the examples show the structure as being used as a type and not as a property that looks something like this:

```
struct Products
{
    public string ProductID;
    public string ProductName;

};
```

The problem is, all you are doing with a structure in C# is making a bunch of names equal to a value type – such as a string – but not creating a named value pair. Put another way, the structure was not based on a property collection but a collection of types – such as a string.

The class, as show below, is doing it right. Meaning the pair of name and value are in property format. So, no matter how you wrote the code for the grid to show both name and value, all you would get is the Name:

```
struct Products
{
    public string ProductID { get; set; }
    public string ProductName { get; set; }

};
```

```
GridView gv = new GridView();
Binding bi = null;
GridViewColumn c = null;

bi = new Binding("ProductID");
c = new GridViewColumn();
c.Header = "ProductID";
c.DisplayMemberBinding = bi;
gv.Columns.Add(c);

bi = new Binding("ProductName");
c = new GridViewColumn();
```

```
c.Header = "ProductName";
c.DisplayMemberBinding = bi;
gv.Columns.Add(c);


Products pro = new Products();
pro.ProductID = "1";
pro.ProductName = "Peanut Brittle";

ObservableCollection<Products> Rows = new
ObservableCollection<Products>();
Rows.Add(pro);

listView1.View = gv;
listView1.DataContext = Rows;
```

Comes out looking like this:

AUTOMATING THE PROCESS FOR A MORE POSITIVE PROGRAMMING EXPERIENCE

So far, the majority of the efforts we've put into populating the WPF ListView has been manually. But what if you wanted to create a ListView view of all the published products installed on your computer or someone else's?

That could wind up not only being a large order, without some sort of automation plan in place, it could take you a good solid day to get all the columns and bindings correctly named set.

Why not do it in less than a minute. In fact. Let's do them first. Below is the code:

```
using System;
using System.Collections.Generic;
using System.ComponentModel;
using System.Data;
using System.Drawing;
using System.Linq;
using System.Text;
using System.Windows.Forms;
using Scripting;
using WbemScripting;

namespace WindowsFormsApplication3
{
```

```csharp
public partial class Form1 : Form
{
    public Form1()
    {
        InitializeComponent();
    }

    private void Form1_Load(object sender, EventArgs e)
    {
        SWbemLocator l = new SWbemLocator();
        SWbemServices svc = l.ConnectServer("LocalHost",
"root\\cimv2", "", "", "MS_409", "", 128, null);
        svc.Security_.AuthenticationLevel =
WbemAuthenticationLevelEnum.wbemAuthenticationLevelPktPrivacy;
        svc.Security_.ImpersonationLevel =
WbemImpersonationLevelEnum.wbemImpersonationLevelImpersonate;
        SWbemObject ob = svc.Get("Win32_Product");

        FileSystemObject fso = new FileSystemObject();
        TextStream txtstream =
fso.OpenTextFile(Application.StartupPath + "\\Products.txt",
IOMode.ForWriting, true, Tristate.TristateUseDefault);
        txtstream.WriteLine("          <ListView
Height=\"Auto\" HorizontalAlignment=\"Stretch\"
Name=\"listView1\" VerticalAlignment=\"Stretch\" Width=\"Auto\"
ItemsSource=\"{Binding}\">");
        txtstream.WriteLine("            <ListView.View>");
        txtstream.WriteLine("              <GridView>");

        foreach(SWbemProperty prop in ob.Properties_)
        {
            txtstream.WriteLine("
<GridViewColumn Header=\"" + prop.Name + "\"
DisplayMemberBinding=\"{Binding " + prop.Name +
"}\"></GridViewColumn>");
        }
        txtstream.WriteLine("              </GridView>");
        txtstream.WriteLine("            </ListView.View>");
        txtstream.WriteLine("        </ListView>");
        txtstream.Close();

        txtstream = fso.OpenTextFile(Application.StartupPath
+ "\\structProducts.txt", IOMode.ForWriting, true,
Tristate.TristateUseDefault);
        txtstream.WriteLine("    struct Products");
```

```
            txtstream.WriteLine("     {");
            foreach (SWbemProperty prop in ob.Properties_)
            {
                txtstream.WriteLine("          public string " +
prop.Name + " { get; set; }");
            }
            txtstream.WriteLine("     };");
            txtstream.Close();

            txtstream = fso.OpenTextFile(Application.StartupPath
+ "\\EnumProducts.txt", IOMode.ForWriting, true,
Tristate.TristateUseDefault);

            txtstream.WriteLine("
ObservableCollection<Products> Rows = new
ObservableCollection<Products>();");
            txtstream.WriteLine("          SWbemLocator l = new
SWbemLocator();");
            txtstream.WriteLine("          SWbemServices svc =
l.ConnectServer(\"LocalHost\", \"root\\\\cimv2\", \"\", \"\",
\"MS_409\", \"\", 128, null);");
            txtstream.WriteLine("
svc.Security_.AuthenticationLevel =
WbemAuthenticationLevelEnum.wbemAuthenticationLevelPktPrivacy;");
            txtstream.WriteLine("
svc.Security_.ImpersonationLevel =
WbemImpersonationLevelEnum.wbemImpersonationLevelImpersonate;");
            txtstream.WriteLine("          SWbemObjectSet objs
= svc.InstancesOf(\"Win32_Product\");");
            txtstream.WriteLine("          foreach(SWbemObject
obj in objs)");
            txtstream.WriteLine("          {");
            txtstream.WriteLine("              Products P = new
Products();");
            foreach (SWbemProperty prop in ob.Properties_)
            {
                txtstream.WriteLine("                  P." +
prop.Name + " = GetManagementValue(\"" + prop.Name + "\",
obj);");
            }

            txtstream.WriteLine("              Rows.Add(P);");
            txtstream.WriteLine("          }");
            txtstream.WriteLine("
this.listView1.ItemsSource = Rows;");
```

```
            txtstream.WriteLine("          }");
            txtstream.WriteLine("             private System.String
GetManagementValue(System.String Name, SWbemObject mo)");
            txtstream.WriteLine("          {");
            txtstream.WriteLine("              int pos = 0;");
            txtstream.WriteLine("              System.String tName
= Name + \" = \";");
            txtstream.WriteLine("              System.String
tempstr = mo.GetObjectText_(0);");
            txtstream.WriteLine("              pos =
tempstr.IndexOf(tName);");
            txtstream.WriteLine("              if (pos > -1)");
            txtstream.WriteLine("              {");
            txtstream.WriteLine("                pos = pos +
tName.Length;");
            txtstream.WriteLine("                tempstr =
tempstr.Substring(pos, tempstr.Length - pos);");
            txtstream.WriteLine("                pos =
tempstr.IndexOf(\";\");");
            txtstream.WriteLine("                tempstr =
tempstr.Substring(0, pos);");
            txtstream.WriteLine("                tempstr =
tempstr.Replace(\"\\\"\", \"\");");
            txtstream.WriteLine("                tempstr =
tempstr.Replace(\"{\", \"\");");
            txtstream.WriteLine("                tempstr =
tempstr.Replace(\"}\", \"\");");
            txtstream.WriteLine("
if(tempstr.Length > 14)");
            txtstream.WriteLine("                {");
            txtstream.WriteLine("                  if
(mo.Properties_.Item(Name).CIMType ==
WbemCimtypeEnum.wbemCimtypeDatetime)");
            txtstream.WriteLine("                  {");
            txtstream.WriteLine("                    return
tempstr.Substring(5, 2) + \"/\" + tempstr.Substring(7, 2) + \"/\"
+ tempstr.Substring(0, 4) + \" \" + tempstr.Substring(9, 2) +
\":\" + tempstr.Substring(11, 2) + \":\" + tempstr.Substring(13,
2);");
            txtstream.WriteLine("                  }");
            txtstream.WriteLine("                }");
            txtstream.WriteLine("                return
tempstr;");
            txtstream.WriteLine("              }");
            txtstream.WriteLine("              else");
```

```
            txtstream.WriteLine("                    {");
            txtstream.WriteLine("                        return \"\";");
            txtstream.WriteLine("                    }");
            txtstream.WriteLine("                }");
        }
    }

}
```

The Structure:

```
  struct Products
  {
      public string AssignmentType { get; set; }
      public string Caption { get; set; }
      public string Description { get; set; }
      public string HelpLink { get; set; }
      public string HelpTelephone { get; set; }
      public string IdentifyingNumber { get; set; }
      public string InstallDate { get; set; }
      public string InstallDate2 { get; set; }
      public string InstallLocation { get; set; }
      public string InstallSource { get; set; }
      public string InstallState { get; set; }
      public string Language { get; set; }
      public string LocalPackage { get; set; }
      public string Name { get; set; }
      public string PackageCache { get; set; }
      public string PackageCode { get; set; }
      public string PackageName { get; set; }
      public string ProductID { get; set; }
      public string RegCompany { get; set; }
      public string RegOwner { get; set; }
      public string SKUNumber { get; set; }
      public string Transforms { get; set; }
      public string URLInfoAbout { get; set; }
      public string URLUpdateInfo { get; set; }
      public string Vendor { get; set; }
      public string Version { get; set; }
      public string WordCount { get; set; }
  };
```

The Listview XML:

```
<ListView Height="Auto" HorizontalAlignment="Stretch" Name="listView1"
VerticalAlignment="Stretch" Width="Auto" ItemsSource="{Binding}">
    <ListView.View>
        <GridView>
            <GridViewColumn                    Header="AssignmentType"
DisplayMemberBinding="{Binding AssignmentType}"></GridViewColumn>
            <GridViewColumn Header="Caption" DisplayMemberBinding="{Binding
Caption}"></GridViewColumn>
            <GridViewColumn                    Header="Description"
DisplayMemberBinding="{Binding Description}"></GridViewColumn>
            <GridViewColumn                    Header="HelpLink"
DisplayMemberBinding="{Binding HelpLink}"></GridViewColumn>
            <GridViewColumn                    Header="HelpTelephone"
DisplayMemberBinding="{Binding HelpTelephone}"></GridViewColumn>
            <GridViewColumn                    Header="IdentifyingNumber"
DisplayMemberBinding="{Binding IdentifyingNumber}"></GridViewColumn>
            <GridViewColumn                    Header="InstallDate"
DisplayMemberBinding="{Binding InstallDate}"></GridViewColumn>
            <GridViewColumn                    Header="InstallDate2"
DisplayMemberBinding="{Binding InstallDate2}"></GridViewColumn>
            <GridViewColumn                    Header="InstallLocation"
DisplayMemberBinding="{Binding InstallLocation}"></GridViewColumn>
            <GridViewColumn                    Header="InstallSource"
DisplayMemberBinding="{Binding InstallSource}"></GridViewColumn>
            <GridViewColumn                    Header="InstallState"
DisplayMemberBinding="{Binding InstallState}"></GridViewColumn>
            <GridViewColumn                    Header="Language"
DisplayMemberBinding="{Binding Language}"></GridViewColumn>
            <GridViewColumn                    Header="LocalPackage"
DisplayMemberBinding="{Binding LocalPackage}"></GridViewColumn>
            <GridViewColumn Header="Name" DisplayMemberBinding="{Binding
Name}"></GridViewColumn>
            <GridViewColumn                    Header="PackageCache"
DisplayMemberBinding="{Binding PackageCache}"></GridViewColumn>
            <GridViewColumn                    Header="PackageCode"
DisplayMemberBinding="{Binding PackageCode}"></GridViewColumn>
```

```
            <GridViewColumn                        Header="PackageName"
DisplayMemberBinding="{Binding PackageName}"></GridViewColumn>
            <GridViewColumn                        Header="ProductID"
DisplayMemberBinding="{Binding ProductID}"></GridViewColumn>
            <GridViewColumn                        Header="RegCompany"
DisplayMemberBinding="{Binding RegCompany}"></GridViewColumn>
            <GridViewColumn                        Header="RegOwner"
DisplayMemberBinding="{Binding RegOwner}"></GridViewColumn>
            <GridViewColumn                        Header="SKUNumber"
DisplayMemberBinding="{Binding SKUNumber}"></GridViewColumn>
            <GridViewColumn                        Header="Transforms"
DisplayMemberBinding="{Binding Transforms}"></GridViewColumn>
            <GridViewColumn                        Header="URLInfoAbout"
DisplayMemberBinding="{Binding URLInfoAbout}"></GridViewColumn>
            <GridViewColumn                        Header="URLUpdateInfo"
DisplayMemberBinding="{Binding URLUpdateInfo}"></GridViewColumn>
            <GridViewColumn Header="Vendor" DisplayMemberBinding="{Binding
Vendor}"></GridViewColumn>
            <GridViewColumn Header="Version" DisplayMemberBinding="{Binding
Version}"></GridViewColumn>
            <GridViewColumn                        Header="WordCount"
DisplayMemberBinding="{Binding WordCount}"></GridViewColumn>
        </GridView>
      </ListView.View>
    </ListView>
```

The Code:

```
        ObservableCollection<Products>        Rows        =        new
ObservableCollection<Products>();
        SWbemLocator l = new SWbemLocator();
        SWbemServices svc = l.ConnectServer("LocalHost", "root\\cimv2", "", "",
"MS_409", "", 128, null);
        svc.Security_.AuthenticationLevel                             =
WbemAuthenticationLevelEnum.wbemAuthenticationLevelPktPrivacy;
        svc.Security_.ImpersonationLevel                             =
WbemImpersonationLevelEnum.wbemImpersonationLevelImpersonate;
        SWbemObjectSet objs = svc.InstancesOf("Win32_Product");
        foreach(SWbemObject obj in objs)
        {
```

```
        Products P = new Products();
        P.AssignmentType = GetManagementValue("AssignmentType", obj);
        P.Caption = GetManagementValue("Caption", obj);
        P.Description = GetManagementValue("Description", obj);
        P.HelpLink = GetManagementValue("HelpLink", obj);
        P.HelpTelephone = GetManagementValue("HelpTelephone", obj);
        P.IdentifyingNumber = GetManagementValue("IdentifyingNumber", obj);
        P.InstallDate = GetManagementValue("InstallDate", obj);
        P.InstallDate2 = GetManagementValue("InstallDate2", obj);
        P.InstallLocation = GetManagementValue("InstallLocation", obj);
        P.InstallSource = GetManagementValue("InstallSource", obj);
        P.InstallState = GetManagementValue("InstallState", obj);
        P.Language = GetManagementValue("Language", obj);
        P.LocalPackage = GetManagementValue("LocalPackage", obj);
        P.Name = GetManagementValue("Name", obj);
        P.PackageCache = GetManagementValue("PackageCache", obj);
        P.PackageCode = GetManagementValue("PackageCode", obj);
        P.PackageName = GetManagementValue("PackageName", obj);
        P.ProductID = GetManagementValue("ProductID", obj);
        P.RegCompany = GetManagementValue("RegCompany", obj);
        P.RegOwner = GetManagementValue("RegOwner", obj);
        P.SKUNumber = GetManagementValue("SKUNumber", obj);
        P.Transforms = GetManagementValue("Transforms", obj);
        P.URLInfoAbout = GetManagementValue("URLInfoAbout", obj);
        P.URLUpdateInfo = GetManagementValue("URLUpdateInfo", obj);
        P.Vendor = GetManagementValue("Vendor", obj);
        P.Version = GetManagementValue("Version", obj);
        P.WordCount = GetManagementValue("WordCount", obj);
        Rows.Add(P);
    }
    this.listView1.ItemsSource = Rows;
}
private System.String GetManagementValue(System.String Name, SWbemObject
mo)
{
    int pos = 0;
    System.String tName = Name + " = ";
    System.String tempstr = mo.GetObjectText_(0);
    pos = tempstr.IndexOf(tName);
    if (pos > -1)
```

```csharp
            {
                pos = pos + tName.Length;
                tempstr = tempstr.Substring(pos, tempstr.Length - pos);
                pos = tempstr.IndexOf(";");
                tempstr = tempstr.Substring(0, pos);
                tempstr = tempstr.Replace("\"", "");
                tempstr = tempstr.Replace("{", "");
                tempstr = tempstr.Replace("}", "");
                if(tempstr.Length > 14)
                {
                    if                    (mo.Properties_.Item(Name).CIMType                    ==
WbemCimtypeEnum.wbemCimtypeDatetime)
                    {
                        return tempstr.Substring(5, 2) + "/" + tempstr.Substring(7, 2) + "/" +
tempstr.Substring(0, 4) + " " + tempstr.Substring(9, 2) + ":" + tempstr.Substring(11,
2) + ":" + tempstr.Substring(13, 2);
                    }
                }
                return tempstr;
            }
            else
            {
                return "";
            }
        }
```

The results:

AssignmentType	Caption	Description	
0	Kindle Create Add-in for Microsoft Word	Kindle Create Add-in for Microsoft Word	
1	Microsoft Office 2003 Web Components	Microsoft Office 2003 Web Components	
1	Microsoft Application Error Reporting	Microsoft Application Error Reporting	
1	Office 16 Click-to-Run Extensibility Component	Office 16 Click-to-Run Extensibility Component	
1	Office 16 Click-to-Run Localization Component	Office 16 Click-to-Run Localization Component	
1	Office 16 Click-to-Run Extensibility Component 64-bit Registration	Office 16 Click-to-Run Extensibility Component 64-bit Registration	
1	Office 16 Click-to-Run Licensing Component	Office 16 Click-to-Run Licensing Component	
1	Microsoft .NET Framework 4.5.1 Multi-Targeting Pack	Microsoft .NET Framework 4.5.1 Multi-Targeting Pack	
1	Microsoft Visual C++ 2017 x64 Additional Runtime - 14.15.26706	Microsoft Visual C++ 2017 x64 Additional Runtime - 14.15.26706	
1	SQL Server Report Builder 3 for SQL Server 2012	SQL Server Report Builder 3 for SQL Server 2012	
1	vs_minshellmsi	vs_minshellmsi	
1	Microsoft Visual Studio 2010 ADO.NET Entity Framework Tools	Microsoft Visual Studio 2010 ADO.NET Entity Framework Tools	
1	Microsoft ASP.NET MVC 2	Microsoft ASP.NET MVC 2	
1	Microsoft Visual C++ 2008 Redistributable - x86 9.0.30729.4974	Microsoft Visual C++ 2008 Redistributable - x86 9.0.30729.4974	
1	Kits Configuration Installer	Kits Configuration Installer	
1	vs_FileTracker_Singleton	vs_FileTracker_Singleton	
1	Microsoft Workflow Debugger v1.0 for amd64	Microsoft Workflow Debugger v1.0 for amd64	
1	Microsoft .NET Framework 4.6.1 SDK	Microsoft .NET Framework 4.6.1 SDK	
1	Microsoft .NET Framework 4.7.1 Doc Redirected Targeting Pack (EN	Microsoft .NET Framework 4.7.1 Doc Redirected Targeting Pack (E	
1	Windows SDK Desktop Tools x86	Windows SDK Desktop Tools x86	
1	VS JIT Debugger	VS JIT Debugger	

Also, you can just change the struct to class any you now have a class to use as well.

Now, it is time to roll this into a totally dynamically drive code example.

DYNAMICALLY DRIVEN RUNTIME CODE

Where the impossible becomes possible

The code that we are about to cover is going to make it possible to use any information data engine which has columns and rows and turn that information into content that can be used by the WPF ListView.

Unfortunately, to show you all of the possibilities in one book is impossible. So, I have decided to break each one out into separate books. So, after this chapter – which it and the chapters above will be in all the other books, we are going to be working one of those specific data engines.

With that said, here's the idea. We want to create out columns, the bindings and generate a DataTable in code. Also, because we can do it, this also offers the possibilities of having the information in the ListView viewed in both horizontal and vertical format.

Horizontal Format

```
using System;
using System.Collections.Generic;
using System.Linq;
using System.Text;
using System.Windows;
using System.Windows.Controls;
```

```csharp
using System.Windows.Data;
using System.Windows.Documents;
using System.Windows.Input;
using System.Windows.Media;
using System.Windows.Media.Imaging;
using System.Windows.Shapes;
using System.Data;
using System.Collections.ObjectModel;
using Scripting;
using WbemScripting;

namespace WpfApplication9
{
    /// <summary>
    /// Interaction logic for Window1.xaml
    /// </summary>
    ///
    public partial class MainWindow : Window
    {
        public MainWindow()
        {
            InitializeComponent();

        }

        private void Window_Loaded(object sender, RoutedEventArgs e)
        {


            System.Data.DataTable dt = new System.Data.DataTable();
            GridView gv = new GridView();
            Binding bi = null;
            GridViewColumn c = null;


            SWbemLocator l = new SWbemLocator();
            SWbemServices svc = l.ConnectServer("LocalHost", "root\\cimv2", "", "", "MS_409", "", 128, null);
            svc.Security_.AuthenticationLevel = WbemAuthenticationLevelEnum.wbemAuthenticationLevelPktPrivacy;
            svc.Security_.ImpersonationLevel = WbemImpersonationLevelEnum.wbemImpersonationLevelImpersonate;
```

```
            SWbemObjectSet objs =
svc.InstancesOf("Win32_Process");
            foreach (SWbemObject obj in objs)
            {
                foreach (SWbemProperty prop in obj.Properties_)
                {
                    dt.Columns.Add(prop.Name);
                    bi = new Binding(prop.Name);
                    c = new GridViewColumn();
                    c.Header = prop.Name;
                    c.DisplayMemberBinding = bi;
                    gv.Columns.Add(c);
                }
                break;
            }

            foreach (SWbemObject obj in objs)
            {
                System.Data.DataRow dr = dt.NewRow();

                foreach (SWbemProperty prop in obj.Properties_)
                {
                    dr[prop.Name] = GetManagementValue(prop.Name,
obj);
                }
                dt.Rows.Add(dr);
            }
            listView1.View = gv;
            this.listView1.DataContext = dt;
        }
        private System.String GetManagementValue(System.String
Name, SWbemObject mo)
        {
            int pos = 0;
            System.String tName = Name + " = ";
            System.String tempstr = mo.GetObjectText_(0);
            pos = tempstr.IndexOf(tName);
            if (pos > -1)
            {
                pos = pos + tName.Length;
                tempstr = tempstr.Substring(pos, tempstr.Length -
pos);

                pos = tempstr.IndexOf(";");
                tempstr = tempstr.Substring(0, pos);
                tempstr = tempstr.Replace("\"", "");
```

```csharp
            tempstr = tempstr.Replace("{", "");
            tempstr = tempstr.Replace("}", "");
            if (tempstr.Length > 14)
            {
                if (mo.Properties_.Item(Name).CIMType ==
WbemCimtypeEnum.wbemCimtypeDatetime)
                {
                    return tempstr.Substring(5, 2) + "/" +
tempstr.Substring(7, 2) + "/" + tempstr.Substring(0, 4) + " " +
tempstr.Substring(9, 2) + ":" + tempstr.Substring(11, 2) + ":" +
tempstr.Substring(13, 2);
                }
            }
            return tempstr;
        }
        else
        {
            return "";
        }
    }

    }
}
```

The results:

MainWindow — □ ×

Caption	CommandLine	CreationClassName
System Idle Process		Win32_Process
System		Win32_Process
smss.exe		Win32_Process
csrss.exe		Win32_Process
csrss.exe		Win32_Process
wininit.exe		Win32_Process
winlogon.exe	winlogon.exe	Win32_Process
services.exe		Win32_Process
lsass.exe	C:\\Windows\\system32\\lsass.exe	Win32_Process
svchost.exe	C:\\Windows\\system32\\svchost.exe -k DcomLaunch	Win32_Process
svchost.exe	C:\\Windows\\system32\\svchost.exe -k RPCSS	Win32_Process
dwm.exe	\dwm.exe\	Win32_Process
svchost.exe	C:\\Windows\\System32\\svchost.exe -k termsvcs	Win32_Process
svchost.exe	C:\\Windows\\System32\\svchost.exe -k LocalSystemNetworkRestricted	Win32_Process
svchost.exe	C:\\Windows\\System32\\svchost.exe -k LocalServiceNetworkRestricted	Win32_Process
svchost.exe	C:\\Windows\\system32\\svchost.exe -k LocalServiceNoNetwork	Win32_Process
svchost.exe	C:\\Windows\\system32\\svchost.exe -k LocalService	Win32_Process
WUDFHost.exe	\C:\\Windows\\System32\\WUDFHost.exe\ -HostGUID:193a1820-d9ac--	Win32_Process
NVDisplay.Containe	\C:\\Program Files\\NVIDIA Corporation\\Display.NvContainer\\NVDisp	Win32_Process
svchost.exe	C:\\Windows\\System32\\svchost.exe -k NetworkService	Win32_Process
svchost.exe	C:\\Windows\\System32\\svchost.exe -k netsvcs	Win32_Process
svchost.exe	C:\\Windows\\system32\\svchost.exe -k LocalServiceNetworkRestricted	Win32_Process
svchost.exe	C:\\Windows\\System32\\svchost.exe -k WlansvcGroup	Win32_Process
svchost.exe	C:\\Windows\\system32\\svchost.exe -k LocalServiceNetworkRestricted	Win32_Process

Vertical View

```csharp
using System;
using System.Collections.Generic;
using System.Linq;
using System.Text;
using System.Windows;
using System.Windows.Controls;
using System.Windows.Data;
using System.Windows.Documents;
using System.Windows.Input;
using System.Windows.Media;
using System.Windows.Media.Imaging;
using System.Windows.Shapes;
using System.Data;
```

```csharp
using System.Collections.ObjectModel;
using Scripting;
using WbemScripting;

namespace WpfApplication9
{
    /// <summary>
    /// Interaction logic for Window1.xaml
    /// </summary>
    ///
    public partial class MainWindow : Window
    {
        public MainWindow()
        {
            InitializeComponent();

        }

        private void Window_Loaded(object sender, RoutedEventArgs
e)
        {
            System.Data.DataTable dt = new
System.Data.DataTable();

            GridView gv = new GridView();
            Binding bi = null;
            GridViewColumn c = null;


            SWbemLocator l = new SWbemLocator();
            SWbemServices svc = l.ConnectServer("LocalHost",
"root\\cimv2", "", "", "MS_409", "", 128, null);
            svc.Security_.AuthenticationLevel =
WbemAuthenticationLevelEnum.wbemAuthenticationLevelPktPrivacy;
            svc.Security_.ImpersonationLevel =
WbemImpersonationLevelEnum.wbemImpersonationLevelImpersonate;
            SWbemObjectSet objs =
svc.InstancesOf("Win32_Process");

            dt.Columns.Add("Property Name");
            bi = new Binding("Property Name");
            c = new GridViewColumn();
            c.Header = "Property Name";
            c.DisplayMemberBinding = bi;
            gv.Columns.Add(c);
```

```
            int y = 0;

            foreach (SWbemObject obj2 in objs)
            {
                dt.Columns.Add("Row" + y);
                bi = new Binding("Row" + y);
                c = new GridViewColumn();
                c.Header = "Row" + y;
                c.DisplayMemberBinding = bi;
                gv.Columns.Add(c);
                y = y + 1;
            }

            SWbemObject obj = objs.ItemIndex(0);
            foreach (SWbemProperty prop in obj.Properties_)
            {
                System.Data.DataRow dr = dt.NewRow();
                dr["Property Name"] = prop.Name;
                y = 0;
                foreach (SWbemObject obj1 in objs)
                {
                    dr["Row" + y] = GetManagementValue(prop.Name,
obj1);

                    y = y + 1;
                }
                dt.Rows.Add(dr);
            }
            listView1.View = gv;
            this.listView1.DataContext = dt;


        }
        private System.String GetManagementValue(System.String
Name, SWbemObject mo)
        {
            int pos = 0;
            System.String tName = Name + " = ";
            System.String tempstr = mo.GetObjectText_(0);
            pos = tempstr.IndexOf(tName);
            if (pos > -1)
            {
                pos = pos + tName.Length;
                tempstr = tempstr.Substring(pos, tempstr.Length -
pos);
```

```
            pos = tempstr.IndexOf(";");
            tempstr = tempstr.Substring(0, pos);
            tempstr = tempstr.Replace("\"", "");
            tempstr = tempstr.Replace("{", "");
            tempstr = tempstr.Replace("}", "");
            if (tempstr.Length > 14)
            {
                if (mo.Properties_.Item(Name).CIMType ==
WbemCimtypeEnum.wbemCimtypeDatetime)
                {
                    return tempstr.Substring(5, 2) + "/" +
tempstr.Substring(7, 2) + "/" + tempstr.Substring(0, 4) + " " +
tempstr.Substring(9, 2) + ":" + tempstr.Substring(11, 2) + ":" +
tempstr.Substring(13, 2);
                }
            }
            return tempstr;
        }
        else
        {
            return "";
        }
    }

}
}
```

Results:

Property Name	Row0	Row1	
Caption	System Idle Process	System	smss.exe
CommandLine			
CreationClassName	Win32_Process	Win32_Process	Win32_Pr
CreationDate	82/92/2018 32:90:9.	82/92/2018 32:90:9.	82/92/20
CSCreationClassName	Win32_ComputerSystem	Win32_ComputerSystem	Win32_Cc
CSName	WIN-QM2FHP9BMJG	WIN-QM2FHP9BMJG	WIN-QM:
Description	System Idle Process	System	smss.exe
ExecutablePath			
ExecutionState			
Handle	0	4	336
HandleCount	0	1174	51
InstallDate			
KernelModeTime	4457308125000	7472500000	937500

Now it is time for the main course!

INTERACTING WITH WMI

A deep dive

The nice thing about WMI is it is free, on your machine and there are 12,000 classes that you can call upon. To use then. Only problem is, you have to know where to look.

```
namespace WindowsFormsApplication2
{
    partial class Form1
    {
        /// <summary>
        /// Required designer variable.
        /// </summary>
        private System.ComponentModel.IContainer components =
null;

        /// <summary>
        /// Clean up any resources being used.
        /// </summary>
        /// <param name="disposing">true if managed resources
should be disposed; otherwise, false.</param>
        protected override void Dispose(bool disposing)
        {
            if (disposing && (components != null))
            {
                components.Dispose();
```

```csharp
        }
        base.Dispose(disposing);
    }

    #region Windows Form Designer generated code

    /// <summary>
    /// Required method for Designer support - do not modify
    /// the contents of this method with the code editor.
    /// </summary>
    private void InitializeComponent()
    {
        this.statusStrip1 = new
System.Windows.Forms.StatusStrip();
        this.toolStrip1 = new
System.Windows.Forms.ToolStrip();
        this.toolStrip2 = new
System.Windows.Forms.ToolStrip();
        this.splitContainer1 = new
System.Windows.Forms.SplitContainer();
        this.toolStripLabel1 = new
System.Windows.Forms.ToolStripLabel();
        this.toolStripComboBox1 = new
System.Windows.Forms.ToolStripComboBox();
        this.toolStripLabel2 = new
System.Windows.Forms.ToolStripLabel();
        this.toolStripComboBox2 = new
System.Windows.Forms.ToolStripComboBox();
        this.treeView1 = new System.Windows.Forms.TreeView();
        this.comboBox1 = new System.Windows.Forms.ComboBox();
        this.listViewView1 = new
System.Windows.Forms.ListViewView();
        this.Column1 = new
System.Windows.Forms.ListViewViewTextBoxColumn();
        this.Column2 = new
System.Windows.Forms.ListViewViewTextBoxColumn();
        this.Column3 = new
System.Windows.Forms.ListViewViewTextBoxColumn();
        this.toolStrip1.SuspendLayout();
        this.toolStrip2.SuspendLayout();

((System.ComponentModel.ISupportInitialize)(this.splitContainer1)
).BeginInit();
        this.splitContainer1.Panel1.SuspendLayout();
        this.splitContainer1.Panel2.SuspendLayout();
```

```
            this.splitContainer1.SuspendLayout();

((System.ComponentModel.ISupportInitialize)(this.listViewView1)).
BeginInit();
            this.SuspendLayout();
            //
            // statusStrip1
            //
            this.statusStrip1.Location = new
System.Drawing.Point(0, 563);
            this.statusStrip1.Name = "statusStrip1";
            this.statusStrip1.Size = new System.Drawing.Size(804,
22);
            this.statusStrip1.TabIndex = 0;
            this.statusStrip1.Text = "statusStrip1";
            //
            // toolStrip1
            //
            this.toolStrip1.Items.AddRange(new
System.Windows.Forms.ToolStripItem[] {
            this.toolStripLabel1,
            this.toolStripComboBox1});
            this.toolStrip1.Location = new
System.Drawing.Point(0, 0);
            this.toolStrip1.Name = "toolStrip1";
            this.toolStrip1.Size = new System.Drawing.Size(804,
25);
            this.toolStrip1.TabIndex = 1;
            this.toolStrip1.Text = "toolStrip1";
            //
            // toolStrip2
            //
            this.toolStrip2.Items.AddRange(new
System.Windows.Forms.ToolStripItem[] {
            this.toolStripLabel2,
            this.toolStripComboBox2});
            this.toolStrip2.Location = new
System.Drawing.Point(0, 25);
            this.toolStrip2.Name = "toolStrip2";
            this.toolStrip2.Size = new System.Drawing.Size(804,
25);
            this.toolStrip2.TabIndex = 2;
            this.toolStrip2.Text = "toolStrip2";
            //
            // splitContainer1
```

```
            //
            this.splitContainer1.Dock =
System.Windows.Forms.DockStyle.Fill;
            this.splitContainer1.Location = new
System.Drawing.Point(0, 50);
            this.splitContainer1.Name = "splitContainer1";
            //
            // splitContainer1.Panel1
            //

this.splitContainer1.Panel1.Controls.Add(this.comboBox1);

this.splitContainer1.Panel1.Controls.Add(this.treeView1);
            //
            // splitContainer1.Panel2
            //

this.splitContainer1.Panel2.Controls.Add(this.listViewView1);
            this.splitContainer1.Size = new
System.Drawing.Size(804, 513);
            this.splitContainer1.SplitterDistance = 268;
            this.splitContainer1.TabIndex = 3;
            //
            // toolStripLabel1
            //
            this.toolStripLabel1.Name = "toolStripLabel1";
            this.toolStripLabel1.Size = new
System.Drawing.Size(77, 22);
            this.toolStripLabel1.Text = "Namespaces:";
            //
            // toolStripComboBox1
            //
            this.toolStripComboBox1.AutoSize = false;
            this.toolStripComboBox1.Items.AddRange(new object[] {
            "*Select a Namespace*"});
            this.toolStripComboBox1.Name = "toolStripComboBox1";
            this.toolStripComboBox1.Size = new
System.Drawing.Size(400, 25);
            this.toolStripComboBox1.Sorted = true;
            this.toolStripComboBox1.Text = "*Select a
Namespace*";
            this.toolStripComboBox1.SelectedIndexChanged += new
System.EventHandler(this.toolStripComboBox1_SelectedIndexChanged)
;
            //
```

```
            // toolStripLabel2
            //
            this.toolStripLabel2.AutoSize = false;
            this.toolStripLabel2.Name = "toolStripLabel2";
            this.toolStripLabel2.Size = new
System.Drawing.Size(77, 22);
            this.toolStripLabel2.Text = "Categories:";
            this.toolStripLabel2.TextAlign =
System.Drawing.ContentAlignment.MiddleRight;
            //
            // toolStripComboBox2
            //
            this.toolStripComboBox2.AutoSize = false;
            this.toolStripComboBox2.Items.AddRange(new object[] {
            "*Select a Category*"});
            this.toolStripComboBox2.Name = "toolStripComboBox2";
            this.toolStripComboBox2.Size = new
System.Drawing.Size(400, 23);
            this.toolStripComboBox2.Sorted = true;
            this.toolStripComboBox2.Text = "*Select a Category*";
            this.toolStripComboBox2.SelectedIndexChanged += new
System.EventHandler(this.toolStripComboBox2_SelectedIndexChanged)
;
            //
            // treeView1
            //
            this.treeView1.Dock =
System.Windows.Forms.DockStyle.Fill;
            this.treeView1.Location = new System.Drawing.Point(0,
0);
            this.treeView1.Name = "treeView1";
            this.treeView1.Size = new System.Drawing.Size(268,
513);
            this.treeView1.TabIndex = 0;
            this.treeView1.AfterSelect += new
System.Windows.Forms.TreeViewEventHandler(this.treeView1_AfterSel
ect);
            //
            // comboBox1
            //
            this.comboBox1.FormattingEnabled = true;
            this.comboBox1.Location = new
System.Drawing.Point(12, 57);
            this.comboBox1.Name = "comboBox1";
```

```
            this.comboBox1.Size = new System.Drawing.Size(224,
21);
            this.comboBox1.Sorted = true;
            this.comboBox1.TabIndex = 0;
            this.comboBox1.Visible = false;
            //
            // listViewView1
            //
            this.listViewView1.AutoSizeColumnsMode =
System.Windows.Forms.ListViewViewAutoSizeColumnsMode.AllCells;
            this.listViewView1.ColumnHeadersHeightSizeMode =
System.Windows.Forms.ListViewViewColumnHeadersHeightSizeMode.Auto
Size;
            this.listViewView1.Columns.AddRange(new
System.Windows.Forms.ListViewViewColumn[] {
            this.Column1,
            this.Column2,
            this.Column3});
            this.listViewView1.Dock =
System.Windows.Forms.DockStyle.Fill;
            this.listViewView1.Location = new
System.Drawing.Point(0, 0);
            this.listViewView1.Name = "listViewView1";
            this.listViewView1.Size = new
System.Drawing.Size(532, 513);
            this.listViewView1.TabIndex = 0;
            //
            // Column1
            //
            this.Column1.HeaderText = "Property Name";
            this.Column1.Name = "Column1";
            this.Column1.Width = 102;
            //
            // Column2
            //
            this.Column2.HeaderText = "CIMType";
            this.Column2.Name = "Column2";
            this.Column2.Width = 75;
            //
            // Column3
            //
            this.Column3.HeaderText = "Description";
            this.Column3.Name = "Column3";
            this.Column3.Width = 85;
            //
```

```
            // Form1
            //
            this.AutoScaleDimensions = new
System.Drawing.SizeF(6F, 13F);
            this.AutoScaleMode =
System.Windows.Forms.AutoScaleMode.Font;
            this.ClientSize = new System.Drawing.Size(804, 585);
            this.Controls.Add(this.splitContainer1);
            this.Controls.Add(this.toolStrip2);
            this.Controls.Add(this.toolStrip1);
            this.Controls.Add(this.statusStrip1);
            this.Name = "Form1";
            this.Text = "Form1";
            this.Load += new
System.EventHandler(this.Form1_Load);
            this.toolStrip1.ResumeLayout(false);
            this.toolStrip1.PerformLayout();
            this.toolStrip2.ResumeLayout(false);
            this.toolStrip2.PerformLayout();
            this.splitContainer1.Panel1.ResumeLayout(false);
            this.splitContainer1.Panel2.ResumeLayout(false);

((System.ComponentModel.ISupportInitialize)(this.splitContainer1)
).EndInit();
            this.splitContainer1.ResumeLayout(false);

((System.ComponentModel.ISupportInitialize)(this.listViewView1)).
EndInit();
            this.ResumeLayout(false);
            this.PerformLayout();

        }

        #endregion

        private System.Windows.Forms.StatusStrip statusStrip1;
        private System.Windows.Forms.ToolStrip toolStrip1;
        private System.Windows.Forms.ToolStripLabel
toolStripLabel1;
        private System.Windows.Forms.ToolStripComboBox
toolStripComboBox1;
        private System.Windows.Forms.ToolStrip toolStrip2;
        private System.Windows.Forms.ToolStripLabel
toolStripLabel2;
```

```
        private System.Windows.Forms.ToolStripComboBox
toolStripComboBox2;
        private System.Windows.Forms.SplitContainer
splitContainer1;
        private System.Windows.Forms.TreeView treeView1;
        private System.Windows.Forms.ComboBox comboBox1;
        private System.Windows.Forms.ListViewView listViewView1;
        private System.Windows.Forms.ListViewViewTextBoxColumn
Column1;
        private System.Windows.Forms.ListViewViewTextBoxColumn
Column2;
        private System.Windows.Forms.ListViewViewTextBoxColumn
Column3;
    }
}
```

The form:

```
using System;
using System.Collections.Generic;
using System.ComponentModel;
using System.Data;
using System.Drawing;
using System.Linq;
using System.Text;
using System.Windows.Forms;
using WbemScripting;
using Scripting;

namespace WindowsFormsApplication2
{
    public partial class Form1 : Form
    {
        public Form1()
        {
            InitializeComponent();
        }

        private void Form1_Load(object sender, EventArgs e)
        {
            EnumNamespaces("root");

        }
```

```csharp
private void EnumNamespaces(string ns)
{
    toolStripComboBox1.Items.Add(ns);
    SWbemLocator l = new SWbemLocator();
    SWbemServices svc = l.ConnectServer("LocalHost", ns,
"", "", "MS_409", "", 128, null);
    svc.Security_.AuthenticationLevel =
WbemAuthenticationLevelEnum.wbemAuthenticationLevelPktPrivacy;
    svc.Security_.ImpersonationLevel =
WbemImpersonationLevelEnum.wbemImpersonationLevelImpersonate;
    try
    {
        SWbemObjectSet objs =
svc.InstancesOf("__NAMESPACE");
        foreach (SWbemObject obj in objs)
        {
            String n = obj.GetType().InvokeMember("Name",
System.Reflection.BindingFlags.GetProperty, null, obj,
null).ToString();
            EnumNamespaces(ns + "\\" + n);
        }
    }
    catch (Exception ex)
    {
        Console.Out.WriteLine(ex.Message);
    }

}

private void
toolStripComboBox1_SelectedIndexChanged(object sender, EventArgs
e)
{
    if (toolStripComboBox1.Text != "*Select a
Namespace*")
    {
        toolStripComboBox2.Items.Clear();

        Scripting.Dictionary odic = new
Scripting.Dictionary();

        SWbemLocator l = new SWbemLocator();
        SWbemServices svc = l.ConnectServer("LocalHost",
toolStripComboBox1.Text, "", "", "MS_409", "", 128, null);
```

```csharp
                svc.Security_.AuthenticationLevel =
WbemAuthenticationLevelEnum.wbemAuthenticationLevelPktPrivacy;
                svc.Security_.ImpersonationLevel =
WbemImpersonationLevelEnum.wbemImpersonationLevelImpersonate;
                try
                {
                    SWbemObjectSet objs = svc.SubclassesOf();

                    foreach (SWbemObject obj in objs)
                    {
                        if (obj.Properties_.Count > 2)
                        {
                            int pos =
obj.Path_.Class.IndexOf("_");

                            switch (pos)
                            {

                                case -1:

                                    if
(odic.Exists(obj.Path_.Class) == false)
                                    {

toolStripComboBox2.Items.Add(obj.Path_.Class);
                                        odic.Add(obj.Path_.Class,
obj.Path_.Class);
                                    }
                                    break;
                                case 0:
                                    if
(odic.Exists("SuperClasses") == false)
                                    {

toolStripComboBox2.Items.Add("SuperClasses");
                                        odic.Add("SuperClasses",
"SuperClasses");
                                    }
                                    break;
                                default:
                                    if
(odic.Exists(obj.Path_.Class.Substring(0, pos)) == false)
                                    {

toolStripComboBox2.Items.Add(obj.Path_.Class.Substring(0, pos));
```

```
odic.Add(obj.Path_.Class.Substring(0, pos),
obj.Path_.Class.Substring(0, pos));
                                    }
                                        break;
                            }

                    }

                }
            }
            catch (Exception ex)
            {
                Console.Out.WriteLine(ex.Message);
            }

        }
    }

        private void treeView1_AfterSelect(object sender,
TreeViewEventArgs e)
        {
            listViewView1.Rows.Clear();
            int y = 0;

            SWbemLocator l = new SWbemLocator();
            SWbemServices svc = l.ConnectServer("LocalHost",
toolStripComboBox1.Text, "", "", "MS_409", "", 128, null);
            svc.Security_.AuthenticationLevel =
WbemAuthenticationLevelEnum.wbemAuthenticationLevelPktPrivacy;
            svc.Security_.ImpersonationLevel =
WbemImpersonationLevelEnum.wbemImpersonationLevelImpersonate;
            SWbemObject obj =
svc.Get(treeView1.SelectedNode.Text.ToString(), 131072, null);
            foreach (SWbemProperty prop in obj.Properties_)
            {
                try
                {
                    listViewView1.Rows.Add();
                    listViewView1.Rows[y].Cells[0].Value =
prop.Name;
                    listViewView1.Rows[y].Cells[1].Value =
prop.Qualifiers_.Item("CIMTYPE").get_Value();
                    listViewView1.Rows[y].Cells[2].Value =
prop.Qualifiers_.Item("Description").get_Value();
```

```csharp
            }
            catch (Exception ex)
            {

            }
            y = y + 1;
        }

    }

    private void
toolStripComboBox2_SelectedIndexChanged(object sender, EventArgs
e)
    {
        if (toolStripComboBox2.Text == "*Select a Category*")
        {
            return;
        }
        treeView1.Nodes.Clear();
        comboBox1.Items.Clear();

        SWbemLocator l = new SWbemLocator();
        SWbemServices svc = l.ConnectServer("LocalHost",
toolStripComboBox1.Text, "", "", "MS_409", "", 128, null);
        svc.Security_.AuthenticationLevel =
WbemAuthenticationLevelEnum.wbemAuthenticationLevelPktPrivacy;
        svc.Security_.ImpersonationLevel =
WbemImpersonationLevelEnum.wbemImpersonationLevelImpersonate;
        try
        {
            SWbemObjectSet objs = svc.SubclassesOf();

            foreach (SWbemObject obj in objs)
            {
                if (obj.Properties_.Count > 2)
                {

                    int pos = obj.Path_.Class.IndexOf("_");

                    switch (pos)
                    {

                        case -1:
```

```csharp
                                    if (toolStripComboBox2.Text ==
obj.Path_.Class)
                                    {

comboBox1.Items.Add(obj.Path_.Class);
                                    }
                                    break;
                                case 0:
                                    if (toolStripComboBox2.Text ==
"SuperClasses")
                                    {

comboBox1.Items.Add(obj.Path_.Class);
                                    }
                                    break;
                                default:
                                    if (toolStripComboBox2.Text ==
obj.Path_.Class.Substring(0, pos))
                                    {

comboBox1.Items.Add(obj.Path_.Class);
                                    }
                                    break;
                            }

                        }

                    }

                    for (int x = 0; x < comboBox1.Items.Count; x++)
                    {

treeView1.Nodes.Add(comboBox1.Items[x].ToString());
                    }

                }
                catch (Exception ex)
                {
                    Console.Out.WriteLine(ex.Message);
                }
            }
        }
}
```

WORKING WITH GET

O f all various interfaces exposed through the SWbemServices, this one is by far the most interesting and informative. If you copied and pasted the code above would see why.

Not only is it capable of providing us with information about what each class does (when provided), it is capable of puling back information we can use to build our views.

Horizontal View

The Code:

```
using System;
using System.Collections.Generic;
using System.Linq;
using System.Text;
using System.Windows;
using System.Windows.Controls;
using System.Windows.Data;
using System.Windows.Documents;
using System.Windows.Input;
using System.Windows.Media;
using System.Windows.Media.Imaging;
using System.Windows.Shapes;
using System.Data;
using System.Collections.ObjectModel;
using Scripting;
using WbemScripting;
```

```csharp
namespace WpfApplication9
{
    /// <summary>
    /// Interaction logic for Window1.xaml
    /// </summary>
    ///
    public partial class MainWindow : Window
    {
        public MainWindow()
        {
            InitializeComponent();

        }

        private void Window_Loaded(object sender, RoutedEventArgs
e)
        {


            System.Data.DataTable dt = new
System.Data.DataTable();
            GridView gv = new GridView();
            Binding bi = null;
            GridViewColumn c = null;


            SWbemLocator l = new SWbemLocator();
            SWbemServices svc = l.ConnectServer("LocalHost",
"root\\cimv2", "", "", "MS_409", "", 128, null);
            svc.Security_.AuthenticationLevel =
WbemAuthenticationLevelEnum.wbemAuthenticationLevelPktPrivacy;
            svc.Security_.ImpersonationLevel =
WbemImpersonationLevelEnum.wbemImpersonationLevelImpersonate;
            SWbemObjectSet objs =
svc.InstancesOf("Win32_Process");
            foreach (SWbemObject obj in objs)
            {
                foreach (SWbemProperty prop in obj.Properties_)
                {
                    dt.Columns.Add(prop.Name);
                    bi = new Binding(prop.Name);
                    c = new GridViewColumn();
                    c.Header = prop.Name;
                    c.DisplayMemberBinding = bi;
```

```
                    gv.Columns.Add(c);
                }
                break;
            }

            foreach (SWbemObject obj in objs)
            {
                System.Data.DataRow dr = dt.NewRow();

                foreach (SWbemProperty prop in obj.Properties_)
                {
                    dr[prop.Name] = GetManagementValue(prop.Name,
obj);
                }
                dt.Rows.Add(dr);
            }
            listView1.View = gv;
            this.listView1.DataContext = dt;
        }
        private System.String GetManagementValue(System.String
Name, SWbemObject mo)
        {
            int pos = 0;
            System.String tName = Name + " = ";
            System.String tempstr = mo.GetObjectText_(0);
            pos = tempstr.IndexOf(tName);
            if (pos > -1)
            {
                pos = pos + tName.Length;
                tempstr = tempstr.Substring(pos, tempstr.Length -
pos);
                pos = tempstr.IndexOf(";");
                tempstr = tempstr.Substring(0, pos);
                tempstr = tempstr.Replace("\"", "");
                tempstr = tempstr.Replace("{", "");
                tempstr = tempstr.Replace("}", "");
                if (tempstr.Length > 14)
                {
                    if (mo.Properties_.Item(Name).CIMType ==
WbemCimtypeEnum.wbemCimtypeDatetime)
                    {
                        return tempstr.Substring(5, 2) + "/" +
tempstr.Substring(7, 2) + "/" + tempstr.Substring(0, 4) + " " +
tempstr.Substring(9, 2) + ":" + tempstr.Substring(11, 2) + ":" +
tempstr.Substring(13, 2);
```

```
                }
            }
            return tempstr;
        }
        else
        {
            return "";
        }
    }
}
```

The results:

Vertical View

The code:

```csharp
using System;
using System.Collections.Generic;
using System.Linq;
using System.Text;
using System.Windows;
using System.Windows.Controls;
using System.Windows.Data;
using System.Windows.Documents;
using System.Windows.Input;
using System.Windows.Media;
using System.Windows.Media.Imaging;
using System.Windows.Shapes;
using System.Data;
using System.Collections.ObjectModel;
using Scripting;
using WbemScripting;

namespace WpfApplication9
{
    /// <summary>
    /// Interaction logic for Window1.xaml
    /// </summary>
    ///
    public partial class MainWindow : Window
    {
        public MainWindow()
        {
            InitializeComponent();

        }

        private void Window_Loaded(object sender, RoutedEventArgs
e)
        {


            System.Data.DataTable dt = new
System.Data.DataTable();
            GridView gv = new GridView();
            Binding bi = null;
            GridViewColumn c = null;


            SWbemLocator l = new SWbemLocator();
```

```
SWbemServices svc = l.ConnectServer("LocalHost",
"root\\cimv2", "", "", "MS_409", "", 128, null);
        svc.Security_.AuthenticationLevel =
WbemAuthenticationLevelEnum.wbemAuthenticationLevelPktPrivacy;
        svc.Security_.ImpersonationLevel =
WbemImpersonationLevelEnum.wbemImpersonationLevelImpersonate;
        SWbemObject ob = svc.Get("Win32_Process");
        SWbemObjectSet objs = ob.Instances_(0);

        dt.Columns.Add("Property Name");
        bi = new Binding("Property Name");
        c = new GridViewColumn();
        c.Header = "Property Name";
        c.DisplayMemberBinding = bi;
        gv.Columns.Add(c);

        int y = 0;

        foreach (SWbemObject obj2 in objs)
        {
                dt.Columns.Add("Row" + y);
                bi = new Binding("Row" + y);
                c = new GridViewColumn();
                c.Header = "Row" + y;
                c.DisplayMemberBinding = bi;
                gv.Columns.Add(c);
                y = y + 1;
        }

        SWbemObject obj = objs.ItemIndex(0);
        foreach (SWbemProperty prop in obj.Properties_)
        {
            System.Data.DataRow dr = dt.NewRow();
            dr["Property Name"] = prop.Name;
            y = 0;
            foreach (SWbemObject obj1 in objs)
            {
                dr["Row" + y] = GetManagementValue(prop.Name,
obj1);
                y = y + 1;
            }
            dt.Rows.Add(dr);
        }
        listView1.View = gv;
        this.listView1.DataContext = dt;
```

```csharp
        }
        private System.String GetManagementValue(System.String
Name, SWbemObject mo)
        {
            int pos = 0;
            System.String tName = Name + " = ";
            System.String tempstr = mo.GetObjectText_(0);
            pos = tempstr.IndexOf(tName);
            if (pos > -1)
            {
                pos = pos + tName.Length;
                tempstr = tempstr.Substring(pos, tempstr.Length -
pos);

                pos = tempstr.IndexOf(";");
                tempstr = tempstr.Substring(0, pos);
                tempstr = tempstr.Replace("\"", "");
                tempstr = tempstr.Replace("{", "");
                tempstr = tempstr.Replace("}", "");
                if (tempstr.Length > 14)
                {
                    if (mo.Properties_.Item(Name).CIMType ==
WbemCimtypeEnum.wbemCimtypeDatetime)
                    {
                        return tempstr.Substring(5, 2) + "/" +
tempstr.Substring(7, 2) + "/" + tempstr.Substring(0, 4) + " " +
tempstr.Substring(9, 2) + ":" + tempstr.Substring(11, 2) + ":" +
tempstr.Substring(13, 2);
                    }
                }
                return tempstr;
            }
            else
            {
                return "";
            }
        }

    }
}

Results:
```

Property Name	Row0	Row1	
Caption	System Idle Process	System	smss.exe
CommandLine			
CreationClassName	Win32_Process	Win32_Process	Win32_Pr
CreationDate	82/92/2018 32:90:9.	82/92/2018 32:90:9.	82/92/20
CSCreationClassName	Win32_ComputerSystem	Win32_ComputerSystem	Win32_Cc
CSName	WIN-QM2FHP9BMJG	WIN-QM2FHP9BMJG	WIN-QM:
Description	System Idle Process	System	smss.exe
ExecutablePath			
ExecutionState			
Handle	0	4	336
HandleCount	0	1174	51
InstallDate			
KernelModeTime	4457308125000	7472500000	937500

WORKING WITH INSTANCESOF

nstancesOf is just the straight on version of get without have to call get and then instances_(0). You just make the call and work with what is returned to you straight on.

Horizontal View

The Code:

```
using System;
using System.Collections.Generic;
using System.Linq;
using System.Text;
using System.Windows;
using System.Windows.Controls;
using System.Windows.Data;
using System.Windows.Documents;
using System.Windows.Input;
using System.Windows.Media;
using System.Windows.Media.Imaging;
```

```csharp
using System.Windows.Shapes;
using System.Data;
using System.Collections.ObjectModel;
using Scripting;
using WbemScripting;

namespace WpfApplication9
{
    /// <summary>
    /// Interaction logic for Window1.xaml
    /// </summary>
    ///
    public partial class MainWindow : Window
    {
        public MainWindow()
        {
            InitializeComponent();

        }

        private void Window_Loaded(object sender, RoutedEventArgs
e)
        {


            System.Data.DataTable dt = new
System.Data.DataTable();
            GridView gv = new GridView();
            Binding bi = null;
            GridViewColumn c = null;


            SWbemLocator l = new SWbemLocator();
            SWbemServices svc = l.ConnectServer("LocalHost",
"root\\cimv2", "", "", "MS_409", "", 128, null);
            svc.Security_.AuthenticationLevel =
WbemAuthenticationLevelEnum.wbemAuthenticationLevelPktPrivacy;
            svc.Security_.ImpersonationLevel =
WbemImpersonationLevelEnum.wbemImpersonationLevelImpersonate;
            SWbemObjectSet objs =
svc.InstancesOf("Win32_Process");
            foreach (SWbemObject obj in objs)
            {
                foreach (SWbemProperty prop in obj.Properties_)
                {
```

```
                dt.Columns.Add(prop.Name);
                bi = new Binding(prop.Name);
                c = new GridViewColumn();
                c.Header = prop.Name;
                c.DisplayMemberBinding = bi;
                gv.Columns.Add(c);
            }
            break;
        }

        foreach (SWbemObject obj in objs)
        {
            System.Data.DataRow dr = dt.NewRow();

            foreach (SWbemProperty prop in obj.Properties_)
            {
                dr[prop.Name] = GetManagementValue(prop.Name,
obj);

            }
            dt.Rows.Add(dr);
        }
        listView1.View = gv;
        this.listView1.DataContext = dt;
    }
    private System.String GetManagementValue(System.String
Name, SWbemObject mo)
    {
        int pos = 0;
        System.String tName = Name + " = ";
        System.String tempstr = mo.GetObjectText_(0);
        pos = tempstr.IndexOf(tName);
        if (pos > -1)
        {
            pos = pos + tName.Length;
            tempstr = tempstr.Substring(pos, tempstr.Length -
pos);

            pos = tempstr.IndexOf(";");
            tempstr = tempstr.Substring(0, pos);
            tempstr = tempstr.Replace("\"", "");
            tempstr = tempstr.Replace("{", "");
            tempstr = tempstr.Replace("}", "");
            if (tempstr.Length > 14)
            {
                if (mo.Properties_.Item(Name).CIMType ==
WbemCimtypeEnum.wbemCimtypeDatetime)
```

```
                {
                    return tempstr.Substring(5, 2) + "/" +
tempstr.Substring(7, 2) + "/" + tempstr.Substring(0, 4) + " " +
tempstr.Substring(9, 2) + ":" + tempstr.Substring(11, 2) + ":" +
tempstr.Substring(13, 2);
                }
            }
            return tempstr;
        }
        else
        {
            return "";
        }
    }

}
}
```

The results:

Caption	CommandLine
System Idle Process	
System	
smss.exe	
csrss.exe	
csrss.exe	
wininit.exe	
winlogon.exe	winlogon.exe
services.exe	
lsass.exe	C:\\Windows\\system32\\lsass.exe
svchost.exe	C:\\Windows\\system32\\svchost.exe -k DcomLaunch
svchost.exe	C:\\Windows\\system32\\svchost.exe -k RPCSS
dwm.exe	\dwm.exe\
svchost.exe	C:\\Windows\\System32\\svchost.exe -k termsvcs

MainWindow — □ ×

Vertical View

The code:

```
using System;
using System.Collections.Generic;
using System.Linq;
using System.Text;
using System.Windows;
using System.Windows.Controls;
using System.Windows.Data;
using System.Windows.Documents;
using System.Windows.Input;
using System.Windows.Media;
using System.Windows.Media.Imaging;
using System.Windows.Shapes;
using System.Data;
using System.Collections.ObjectModel;
using Scripting;
using WbemScripting;

namespace WpfApplication9
{
    /// <summary>
    /// Interaction logic for Window1.xaml
    /// </summary>
    ///
    public partial class MainWindow : Window
    {
        public MainWindow()
        {
            InitializeComponent();

        }

        private void Window_Loaded(object sender, RoutedEventArgs
e)
        {


            System.Data.DataTable dt = new
System.Data.DataTable();
            GridView gv = new GridView();
            Binding bi = null;
```

```
GridViewColumn c = null;


SWbemLocator l = new SWbemLocator();
SWbemServices svc = l.ConnectServer("LocalHost",
"root\\cimv2", "", "", "MS_409", "", 128, null);
svc.Security_.AuthenticationLevel =
WbemAuthenticationLevelEnum.wbemAuthenticationLevelPktPrivacy;
svc.Security_.ImpersonationLevel =
WbemImpersonationLevelEnum.wbemImpersonationLevelImpersonate;
SWbemObjectSet objs =
svc.InstancesOf("Win32_Process");


dt.Columns.Add("Property Name");
bi = new Binding("Property Name");
c = new GridViewColumn();
c.Header = "Property Name";
c.DisplayMemberBinding = bi;
gv.Columns.Add(c);

int y = 0;

foreach (SWbemObject obj2 in objs)
{
        dt.Columns.Add("Row" + y);
        bi = new Binding("Row" + y);
        c = new GridViewColumn();
        c.Header = "Row" + y;
        c.DisplayMemberBinding = bi;
        gv.Columns.Add(c);
        y = y + 1;
}

SWbemObject obj = objs.ItemIndex(0);
foreach (SWbemProperty prop in obj.Properties_)
{
    System.Data.DataRow dr = dt.NewRow();
    dr["Property Name"] = prop.Name;
    y = 0;
    foreach (SWbemObject obj1 in objs)
    {
        dr["Row" + y] = GetManagementValue(prop.Name,
obj1);

        y = y + 1;
```

```
                }
                dt.Rows.Add(dr);
            }
            listView1.View = gv;
            this.listView1.DataContext = dt;
        }
        private System.String GetManagementValue(System.String
Name, SWbemObject mo)
        {
            int pos = 0;
            System.String tName = Name + " = ";
            System.String tempstr = mo.GetObjectText_(0);
            pos = tempstr.IndexOf(tName);
            if (pos > -1)
            {
                pos = pos + tName.Length;
                tempstr = tempstr.Substring(pos, tempstr.Length -
pos);
                pos = tempstr.IndexOf(";");
                tempstr = tempstr.Substring(0, pos);
                tempstr = tempstr.Replace("\"", "");
                tempstr = tempstr.Replace("{", "");
                tempstr = tempstr.Replace("}", "");
                if (tempstr.Length > 14)
                {
                    if (mo.Properties_.Item(Name).CIMType ==
WbemCimtypeEnum.wbemCimtypeDatetime)
                    {
                        return tempstr.Substring(5, 2) + "/" +
tempstr.Substring(7, 2) + "/" + tempstr.Substring(0, 4) + " " +
tempstr.Substring(9, 2) + ":" + tempstr.Substring(11, 2) + ":" +
tempstr.Substring(13, 2);
                    }
                }
                return tempstr;
            }
            else
            {
                return "";
            }
        }

    }
}
```

Results:

Property Name	Row0	Row1	
Caption	System Idle Process	System	smss.exe
CommandLine			
CreationClassName	Win32_Process	Win32_Process	Win32_Pr
CreationDate	82/92/2018 32:90:9.	82/92/2018 32:90:9.	82/92/20
CSCreationClassName	Win32_ComputerSystem	Win32_ComputerSystem	Win32_Cc
CSName	WIN-QM2FHP9BMJG	WIN-QM2FHP9BMJG	WIN-QM.
Description	System Idle Process	System	smss.exe
ExecutablePath			
ExecutionState			
Handle	0	4	336
HandleCount	0	1174	51
InstallDate			
KernelModeTime	4457308125000	7472500000	937500

EXECQUERY

ExecQuery stands out only because you can refine your request. Problems arise calling ExecQuery because the information you want in a specific order doesn't return in that order. This will become apparent when you use the code and see the query specifies the properties in a specific order but returns them in another. Also, adding an additional property, too.

Horizontal View

```
using System;
using System.Collections.Generic;
using System.Linq;
using System.Text;
using System.Windows;
using System.Windows.Controls;
using System.Windows.Data;
using System.Windows.Documents;
using System.Windows.Input;
using System.Windows.Media;
using System.Windows.Media.Imaging;
using System.Windows.Shapes;
using System.Data;
using System.Collections.ObjectModel;
using Scripting;
using WbemScripting;

namespace WpfApplication9
{
    /// <summary>
    /// Interaction logic for Window1.xaml
    /// </summary>
```

```
///
public partial class MainWindow : Window
{
    public MainWindow()
    {
        InitializeComponent();

    }

    private void Window_Loaded(object sender, RoutedEventArgs
e)
    {


        System.Data.DataTable dt = new
System.Data.DataTable();
        GridView gv = new GridView();
        Binding bi = null;
        GridViewColumn c = null;


        SWbemLocator l = new SWbemLocator();
        SWbemServices svc = l.ConnectServer("LocalHost",
"root\\cimv2", "", "", "MS_409", "", 128, null);
        svc.Security_.AuthenticationLevel =
WbemAuthenticationLevelEnum.wbemAuthenticationLevelPktPrivacy;
        svc.Security_.ImpersonationLevel =
WbemImpersonationLevelEnum.wbemImpersonationLevelImpersonate;
        SWbemObjectSet objs = svc.ExecQuery("Select
ProcessID, Caption, ExecutablePath, Description from
Win32_Process", "WQL");
        foreach (SWbemObject obj in objs)
        {
            foreach (SWbemProperty prop in obj.Properties_)
            {
                dt.Columns.Add(prop.Name);
                bi = new Binding(prop.Name);
                c = new GridViewColumn();
                c.Header = prop.Name;
                c.DisplayMemberBinding = bi;
                gv.Columns.Add(c);
            }
            break;
        }
```

```csharp
            foreach (SWbemObject obj in objs)
            {
                System.Data.DataRow dr = dt.NewRow();

                foreach (SWbemProperty prop in obj.Properties_)
                {
                    dr[prop.Name] = GetManagementValue(prop.Name,
obj);
                }
                dt.Rows.Add(dr);
            }
            listView1.View = gv;
            this.listView1.DataContext = dt;
        }
        private System.String GetManagementValue(System.String
Name, SWbemObject mo)
        {
            int pos = 0;
            System.String tName = Name + " = ";
            System.String tempstr = mo.GetObjectText_(0);
            pos = tempstr.IndexOf(tName);
            if (pos > -1)
            {
                pos = pos + tName.Length;
                tempstr = tempstr.Substring(pos, tempstr.Length -
pos);

                pos = tempstr.IndexOf(";");
                tempstr = tempstr.Substring(0, pos);
                tempstr = tempstr.Replace("\"", "");
                tempstr = tempstr.Replace("{", "");
                tempstr = tempstr.Replace("}", "");
                if (tempstr.Length > 14)
                {
                    if (mo.Properties_.Item(Name).CIMType ==
WbemCimtypeEnum.wbemCimtypeDatetime)
                    {
                        return tempstr.Substring(5, 2) + "/" +
tempstr.Substring(7, 2) + "/" + tempstr.Substring(0, 4) + " " +
tempstr.Substring(9, 2) + ":" + tempstr.Substring(11, 2) + ":" +
tempstr.Substring(13, 2);
                    }
                }
                return tempstr;
            }
            else
```

```
            {
                return "";
            }
        }

    }
}
```

View:

Caption	Description	ExecutablePath	Handle	ProcessId
System Idle Process	System Idle Process		0	0
System	System		4	4
smss.exe	smss.exe		336	336
csrss.exe	csrss.exe		500	500
csrss.exe	csrss.exe		612	612
wininit.exe	wininit.exe		636	636
winlogon.exe	winlogon.exe	C:\\Windows\\system32\\winlogon.exe	696	696
services.exe	services.exe		760	760
lsass.exe	lsass.exe	C:\\Windows\\system32\\lsass.exe	776	776
svchost.exe	svchost.exe	C:\\Windows\\system32\\svchost.exe	864	864
svchost.exe	svchost.exe	C:\\Windows\\system32\\svchost.exe	928	928
dwm.exe	dwm.exe	C:\\Windows\\system32\\dwm.exe	1016	1016
svchost.exe	svchost.exe	C:\\Windows\\System32\\svchost.exe	356	356
svchost.exe	svchost.exe	C:\\Windows\\System32\\svchost.exe	8	8
svchost exe	svchost exe	C:\\Windows\\System32\\svchost exe	616	616

Vertical View

```
using System;
using System.Collections.Generic;
using System.Linq;
using System.Text;
using System.Windows;
using System.Windows.Controls;
using System.Windows.Data;
using System.Windows.Documents;
using System.Windows.Input;
using System.Windows.Media;
using System.Windows.Media.Imaging;
```

```csharp
using System.Windows.Shapes;
using System.Data;
using System.Collections.ObjectModel;
using Scripting;
using WbemScripting;

namespace WpfApplication10
{
    /// <summary>
    /// Interaction logic for Window1.xaml
    /// </summary>
    ///
    public partial class MainWindow : Window
    {
        public MainWindow()
        {
            InitializeComponent();

        }

        private void Window_Loaded(object sender, RoutedEventArgs e)
        {
            System.Data.DataTable dt = new
System.Data.DataTable();
            GridView gv = new GridView();
            Binding bi = null;
            GridViewColumn c = null;


            SWbemLocator l = new SWbemLocator();
            SWbemServices svc = l.ConnectServer("LocalHost",
"root\\cimv2", "", "", "MS_409", "", 128, null);
            svc.Security_.AuthenticationLevel =
WbemAuthenticationLevelEnum.wbemAuthenticationLevelPktPrivacy;
            svc.Security_.ImpersonationLevel =
WbemImpersonationLevelEnum.wbemImpersonationLevelImpersonate;
            SWbemObjectSet objs = svc.ExecQuery("Select
ProcessID, Caption, ExecutablePath, Description from
Win32_Process");

            dt.Columns.Add("Property Name");
            bi = new Binding("Property Name");
            c = new GridViewColumn();
            c.Header = "Property Name";
```

```csharp
            c.DisplayMemberBinding = bi;
            gv.Columns.Add(c);

            int y = 0;

            foreach (SWbemObject obj2 in objs)
            {
                dt.Columns.Add("Row" + y);
                bi = new Binding("Row" + y);
                c = new GridViewColumn();
                c.Header = "Row" + y;
                c.DisplayMemberBinding = bi;
                gv.Columns.Add(c);
                y = y + 1;
            }

            SWbemObject obj = objs.ItemIndex(0);
            foreach (SWbemProperty prop in obj.Properties_)
            {
                System.Data.DataRow dr = dt.NewRow();
                dr["Property Name"] = prop.Name;
                y = 0;
                foreach (SWbemObject obj1 in objs)
                {
                    dr["Row" + y] = GetManagementValue(prop.Name,
obj1);

                    y = y + 1;
                }
                dt.Rows.Add(dr);
            }
            listView1.View = gv;
            this.listView1.DataContext = dt;
        }
        private System.String GetManagementValue(System.String
Name, SWbemObject mo)
        {
            int pos = 0;
            System.String tName = Name + " = ";
            System.String tempstr = mo.GetObjectText_(0);
            pos = tempstr.IndexOf(tName);
            if (pos > -1)
            {
                pos = pos + tName.Length;
                tempstr = tempstr.Substring(pos, tempstr.Length -
pos);
```

```csharp
                pos = tempstr.IndexOf(";");
                tempstr = tempstr.Substring(0, pos);
                tempstr = tempstr.Replace("\"", "");
                tempstr = tempstr.Replace("{", "");
                tempstr = tempstr.Replace("}", "");
                if (tempstr.Length > 14)
                {
                    if (mo.Properties_.Item(Name).CIMType ==
WbemCimtypeEnum.wbemCimtypeDatetime)
                    {
                        return tempstr.Substring(5, 2) + "/" +
tempstr.Substring(7, 2) + "/" + tempstr.Substring(0, 4) + " " +
tempstr.Substring(9, 2) + ":" + tempstr.Substring(11, 2) + ":" +
tempstr.Substring(13, 2);
                    }
                }
                return tempstr;
            }
            else
            {
                return "";
            }
        }
    }
}
```

View:

Property Name	Row0	Row1	Row2	Row3	Row4	Row5
Caption	System Idle Process	System	smss.exe	csrss.exe	csrss.exe	wininit.exe
Description	System Idle Process	System	smss.exe	csrss.exe	csrss.exe	wininit.exe
ExecutablePath						
Handle	0	4	336	500	612	636
ProcessId	0	4	336	500	612	636

EXECNOTIFICATIONQUE
RY

xecNotificationQuery uses an event source to track the amount of times you may want to trap for an event. Not all classes are suited for event handling and the most common is, of course, win32_Process.

The three primary instance types are: ___InstanceCreationEvent, ___InstanceDeletionEvent, and ___InstanceModificationEvent. The fourth: ___InstanceOperationEvent which gets fired if any of the three events occurs. To filter what you want, you have to filter for the obj.Path_.Class.

There are two primary concerns here. One, ___InstanceModificationEvent is a very noisy event source. Two, while you can filter for which event fired the event in code, there data being returned doesn't tell. So, you could have 30 events being recorded but from the visualization perspective, they are all from the ___InstanceOperationEvent.

You can add a column at very beginning and add to the row what event occurred. Below is the code that will show you what I mean.

Horizontal View

```
using System;
using System.Collections.Generic;
using System.Linq;
using System.Text;
using System.Windows;
using System.Windows.Controls;
using System.Windows.Data;
using System.Windows.Documents;
```

```
using System.Windows.Input;
using System.Windows.Media;
using System.Windows.Media.Imaging;
using System.Windows.Shapes;
using System.Data;
using System.Collections.ObjectModel;
using Scripting;
using WbemScripting;

namespace WpfApplication9
{
    /// <summary>
    /// Interaction logic for Window1.xaml
    /// </summary>
    ///
    public partial class MainWindow : Window
    {
        public MainWindow()
        {
            InitializeComponent();

        }

        private void Window_Loaded(object sender, RoutedEventArgs
e)
        {


            System.Data.DataTable dt = new
System.Data.DataTable();
            GridView gv = new GridView();
            Binding bi = null;
            GridViewColumn c = null;

            int v = 0;
            int w = 0;

            SWbemLocator l = new SWbemLocator();
            SWbemServices svc = l.ConnectServer("LocalHost",
"root\\cimv2", "", "", "MS_409", "", 128, null);
            svc.Security_.AuthenticationLevel =
WbemAuthenticationLevelEnum.wbemAuthenticationLevelPktPrivacy;
            svc.Security_.ImpersonationLevel =
WbemImpersonationLevelEnum.wbemImpersonationLevelImpersonate;
```

```
            SWbemEventSource es =
svc.ExecNotificationQuery("Select * from __InstanceOperationEvent
within 1 where targetInstance ISA'Win32_Process'");

            dt.Columns.Add("Event Type");
            bi = new Binding("Event Type");
            c = new GridViewColumn();
            c.Header = "Event Type";
            c.DisplayMemberBinding = bi;
            gv.Columns.Add(c);

            while(v < 4)
            {
                SWbemObject ti = es.NextEvent(-1);
                SWbemObject obj =
ti.Properties_.Item("TargetInstance").get_Value();

                if(w == 0)
                {
                    foreach (SWbemProperty prop in
obj.Properties_)
                    {

                        dt.Columns.Add(prop.Name);
                        bi = new Binding(prop.Name);
                        c = new GridViewColumn();
                        c.Header = prop.Name;
                        c.DisplayMemberBinding = bi;
                        gv.Columns.Add(c);
                    }
                    w = 1;
                }


                switch(ti.Path_.Class)
                {
                    case "__InstanceCreationEvent":

                        System.Data.DataRow dr = dt.NewRow();

                        dr["Event Type"] =
"__InstanceCreationEvent";
```

```
                        foreach (SWbemProperty prop in
obj.Properties_)
                        {
                             dr[prop.Name] =
GetManagementValue(prop.Name, obj);
                        }
                        dt.Rows.Add(dr);
                        v = v + 1;
                        break;

                  case "__InstanceDeletionEvent":

                        System.Data.DataRow dr1 = dt.NewRow();

                        dr1["Event Type"] =
"__InstanceDeletionEvent";

                        foreach (SWbemProperty prop in
obj.Properties_)
                        {
                             dr1[prop.Name] =
GetManagementValue(prop.Name, obj);
                        }
                        dt.Rows.Add(dr1);
                        v = v + 1;
                        break;

                  case "__InstanceModificationEvent":

                        //dr["Event Type"] =
"__InstanceModificationEvent";

                        //foreach (SWbemProperty prop in
obj.Properties_)
                        //{
                        //     dr[prop.Name] =
GetManagementValue(prop.Name, obj);
                        //}
                        //dt.Rows.Add(dr);
                        //v = v + 1;

                        break;
                  }

             }
```

```
            listView1.View = gv;
            this.listView1.DataContext = dt;
        }


        private System.String GetManagementValue(System.String
Name, SWbemObject mo)
        {
            int pos = 0;
            System.String tName = Name + " = ";
            System.String tempstr = mo.GetObjectText_(0);
            pos = tempstr.IndexOf(tName);
            if (pos > -1)
            {
                pos = pos + tName.Length;
                tempstr = tempstr.Substring(pos, tempstr.Length -
pos);

                pos = tempstr.IndexOf(";");
                tempstr = tempstr.Substring(0, pos);
                tempstr = tempstr.Replace("\"", "");
                tempstr = tempstr.Replace("{", "");
                tempstr = tempstr.Replace("}", "");
                if (tempstr.Length > 14)
                {
                    if (mo.Properties_.Item(Name).CIMType ==
WbemCimtypeEnum.wbemCimtypeDatetime)
                    {
                        return tempstr.Substring(5, 2) + "/" +
tempstr.Substring(7, 2) + "/" + tempstr.Substring(0, 4) + " " +
tempstr.Substring(9, 2) + ":" + tempstr.Substring(11, 2) + ":" +
tempstr.Substring(13, 2);
                    }
                }
                return tempstr;
            }
            else
            {
                return "";
            }
        }

    }
}

Result:
```

Event Type	Caption	CommandLine	Creation
_InstanceCreationEvent	notepad.exe	\C:\\Windows\\system32\\Notepad.exe\	Win32_
_InstanceDeletionEvent	notepad.exe	\C:\\Windows\\system32\\Notepad.exe\	Win32_
_InstanceCreationEvent	win32calc.exe	\C:\\Windows\\System32\\win32calc.exe\	Win32_
_InstanceCreationEvent	svchost.exe		Win32_

Vertical View

```csharp
using System;
using System.Collections.Generic;
using System.Linq;
using System.Text;
using System.Windows;
using System.Windows.Controls;
using System.Windows.Data;
using System.Windows.Documents;
using System.Windows.Input;
using System.Windows.Media;
using System.Windows.Media.Imaging;
using System.Windows.Shapes;
using System.Data;
using System.Collections.ObjectModel;
using Scripting;
using WbemScripting;

namespace WpfApplication10
{
```

```
/// <summary>
/// Interaction logic for Window1.xaml
/// </summary>
///
public partial class MainWindow : Window
{
    public MainWindow()
    {
        InitializeComponent();

    }

    private void Window_Loaded(object sender, RoutedEventArgs
e)
    {
        System.Data.DataTable dt = new
System.Data.DataTable();
        GridView gv = new GridView();
        Binding bi = null;
        GridViewColumn c = null;


        SWbemLocator l = new SWbemLocator();
        SWbemServices svc = l.ConnectServer("LocalHost",
"root\\cimv2", "", "", "MS_409", "", 128, null);
        svc.Security_.AuthenticationLevel =
WbemAuthenticationLevelEnum.wbemAuthenticationLevelPktPrivacy;
        svc.Security_.ImpersonationLevel =
WbemImpersonationLevelEnum.wbemImpersonationLevelImpersonate;
        SWbemEventSource es =
svc.ExecNotificationQuery("Select * from __InstanceOperationEvent
within 1 where targetInstance ISA 'Win32_Process'");

        dt.Columns.Add("Property Name");
        bi = new Binding("Property Name");
        c = new GridViewColumn();
        c.Header = "Property Name";
        c.DisplayMemberBinding = bi;
        gv.Columns.Add(c);


        for(int y=0;y < 4; y++)
        {
            dt.Columns.Add("Row" + y);
            bi = new Binding("Row" + y);
```

```
                c = new GridViewColumn();
                c.Header = "Row" + y;
                c.DisplayMemberBinding = bi;
                gv.Columns.Add(c);

            }


            int v = 0;
            int w = 0;
            int d = 0;
            int r = 0;

            while (v < 4)
            {
                SWbemObject ti = es.NextEvent(-1);
                SWbemObject obj =
ti.Properties_.Item("TargetInstance").get_Value();

                if (w == 0)
                {
                    System.Data.DataRow dr = dt.NewRow();
                    dr["Property Name"] = "Event Type";
                    dt.Rows.Add(dr);
                    foreach (SWbemProperty prop in
obj.Properties_)
                    {
                        dr = dt.NewRow();
                        dr["Property Name"] = prop.Name;
                        dt.Rows.Add(dr);
                    }
                    w = 1;
                }
                d = 0;
                switch (ti.Path_.Class)
                {
                    case "__InstanceCreationEvent":
                        dt.Rows[d]["Row" + v] =
"__InstanceCreationEvent";
                        d = d + 1;
                        foreach (SWbemProperty prop in
obj.Properties_)
                        {
```

```
                            dt.Rows[d]["Row" + v] =
GetManagementValue(prop.Name, obj);
                        d = d + 1;
                    }
                    v = v + 1;
                    break;

                case "__InstanceDeletionEvent":

                    dt.Rows[d]["Row" + v] =
"__InstanceDeletionEvent";
                    d = d + 1;
                    foreach (SWbemProperty prop in
obj.Properties_)
                    {
                        dt.Rows[d]["Row" + v] =
GetManagementValue(prop.Name, obj);
                        d = d + 1;
                    }
                    v = v + 1;
                    break;

                //case "__InstanceModificationEvent":

                //dt.Rows[d].["Rows" + v] =
"__InstanceModificationEvent";
                //d = d +1;
                //foreach (SWbemProperty prop in
obj.Properties_)
                //{
                //   dt.Rows[d].["Rows" + v] =
GetManagementValue(prop.Name, obj);
                //   d=d+1;
                //}
                //v = v + 1;
                //break;
            }

        }
        listView1.View = gv;
        this.listView1.DataContext = dt;
    }
    private System.String GetManagementValue(System.String
Name, SWbemObject mo)
    {
```

```csharp
            int pos = 0;
            System.String tName = Name + " = ";
            System.String tempstr = mo.GetObjectText_(0);
            pos = tempstr.IndexOf(tName);
            if (pos > -1)
            {
                pos = pos + tName.Length;
                tempstr = tempstr.Substring(pos, tempstr.Length -
pos);
                pos = tempstr.IndexOf(";");
                tempstr = tempstr.Substring(0, pos);
                tempstr = tempstr.Replace("\"", "");
                tempstr = tempstr.Replace("{", "");
                tempstr = tempstr.Replace("}", "");
                if (tempstr.Length > 14)
                {
                    if (mo.Properties_.Item(Name).CIMType ==
WbemCimtypeEnum.wbemCimtypeDatetime)
                    {
                        return tempstr.Substring(5, 2) + "/" +
tempstr.Substring(7, 2) + "/" + tempstr.Substring(0, 4) + " " +
tempstr.Substring(9, 2) + ":" + tempstr.Substring(11, 2) + ":" +
tempstr.Substring(13, 2);
                    }
                }
                return tempstr;
            }
            else
            {
                return "";
            }
        }
    }
}
```

The results:

Property Name	Row0	Row1	Row2
Event Type	_InstanceCreationEvent	_InstanceCreationEvent	_InstanceDeletionEvent
Caption	calc.exe	win32calc.exe	calc.exe
CommandLine		\C:\\Windows\\System32\\win32calc.exe\	
CreationClassName	Win32_Process	Win32_Process	Win32_Process
CreationDate	83/01/2018 75:83:1.	83/01/2018 75:83:2.	83/01/2018 75:83:1.
CSCreationClassName	Win32_ComputerSystem	Win32_ComputerSystem	Win32_ComputerSystem
CSName	WIN-QM2FHP9BMJG	WIN-QM2FHP9BMJG	WIN-QM2FHP9BMJG
Description	calc.exe	win32calc.exe	calc.exe
ExecutablePath		C:\\Windows\\System32\\win32calc.exe	
ExecutionState			
Handle	6736	5136	6736
HandleCount	226	131	226
InstallDate			
KernelModeTime	312500	1562500	312500
MaximumWorkingSet!		1380	
MinimumWorkingSetS		200	
Name	Win32_Process	Win32_Process	Win32_Process
OSCreationClassName	Win32_OperatingSystem	Win32_OperatingSystem	Win32_OperatingSystem

So, here we are and at the end of the road. I sincerely hope that the code will help you along your journey as a C# programmer.

www.ingramcontent.com/pod-product-compliance
Lightning Source LLC
Chambersburg PA
CBHW071551080326
40690CB00056B/1794